Getting It:
Building Motivation From Relapse

George Manter DuWors

TABLE OF CONTENTS

ANONYMOUS MAINTENANCE PLAN SCALE: BEFORE

This page is an anonymous survey, designed to collect results for the whole group. It tries to measure how much difference the workbook/group is making overall. You will be asked to choose one "plan" here, after Part I, and again after Part II. An honest answer on this scale will make the workbook better for others over the long haul. Other questions inside the workbook give you a chance to assess and discuss how it is working for you and your group.

Do not put your name on this page---it is meant to be cut out and handed in.

Your counselor may ask you all to put a date or some other mark on the page so s/he knows which group s/he is recording. S/he will calculate only the average numbers for your group.

Below are five possible ways to maintain your own recovery after completing this workbook and any program of which it is a part. Please, circle the one that most closely describes what you are likely to do after you finish the workbook and the program, even if the description is not perfect.

The closest description of my plan to stay clean and sober after completing this program:

1. None. I plan to return to the use of alcohol and/or drugs.

2. Just stay away from drugs and alcohol, using my willpower.

3. Start or resume at least one activity, such as exercise, a nutritional program, a new hobby, or even more time working, to "stay busy" or "keep me going" (without returning to alcohol/drugs). I will not involve myself with any sort of "mutual help" group.

4. Whether I also do parts of number 3 or not, I will attend some sort of "mutual help" meetings until I feel "out of the woods" and able to stay off drugs/alcohol on my own. Or I might participate in some form of psychotherapy until I think I am ready to stay clean and sober on my own. Or I will stay clean and sober solely through my religion, without participation in groups or activities specifically for recovering alcoholic/addicts.

5. Even if I also do some of the above, I will join a 12 Step Program, get a sponsor, work the steps, and attend meetings. If I have already started this, I will continue under the guidance of my sponsor.

CUT HERE

A. Recovery Realizations

Are you tired of starting over?

Are you tired of knowing what the problem is but not solving it?

Are you tired of going in and out of recovery? Tired of relapsing every few weeks, months, or years?

Do you ever wonder what the difference is between you and those who remain clean and sober?

Even if this is your first try at abstinence, would you actually like to be one of those people who just does what needs to be done and remains clean and sober for the rest of his or her life?

If you answer "yes" to even one of these questions, please, consider this: People who successfully work to maintain long-term recovery are doing what they do because it makes sense to them. Just as certainly, this recovery work does not make sense to people who do not do it. When something "makes sense," it fits the only reality we can see, our own. This means that people who continue to work at recovery, long after getting clean and sober, live in a different reality than those who do not. They see something the others do not. They are not "better" or "worse" and neither are you. And most did not get there overnight, often having much treatment and many relapses. But once they settle into lasting recovery, they all seem to share eight realizations about not taking "that first drink/drug." It is the goal of this workbook to help you find those realizations in your own experience and to have them "make sense" to you. Enough sense that you are more willing to try what so many people with lasting recovery do.

This somewhat silly example tries to show how much difference it can make to "get it."

Imagine there is a coffee table between me and my phone. And imagine that I do not realize it is there. The phone rings. I jump up eagerly and rush across the room to answer. Crash! Baffled, I spit out carpet fiber and touch my freshly chipped tooth. But I don't realize why this is happening. The phone rings again. Crash! A sprained elbow. Again. Crash! A laceration.

This keeps happening until one day I lie there and start connecting the dots. "What is going on, what keeps happening?" I ask. I do not see yet, but I am looking. I feel a physical tingling, an excitement. I know there is something. I reach out…Sensation of smoothness, something hard, a bit cool to touch… Holy cow! There is something here: a foot high, solid, eighteen inches wide, seems to have four—…a table! There is a table here! Why didn't someone tell me? (They did, only a hundred times. But I was not "open.")

What difference does my "realization" make? Now that my reality includes the table, it also includes options that had been just as "invisible" to me as the table itself. I can walk around it. Step on or over it. Move it. Smash it with an ax! But none of these practical alternatives was possible until I "realized" the table was there. I just wasn't getting it!

This workbook is for those of you who have tripped a time or two, or twenty, or a hundred. You may know alcohol/drugs are involved, but that has not been enough to stop you from tripping again. The workbook appeals to the part of you that is open to finding a reality you had not previously seen. A part of you that is tired of the sensations of falling down, of being kicked and/or kicking yourself. It offers you a chance to "get" something, something that will offer options like the table did—if you are willing and able to tolerate the sensations of seeing something new about your own relapse experience. Options that prevent you from ever having to trip again. Ready?

B. Two Kinds of Relapse Decision

Definition: For purposes of this workbook, a "relapse" happens when we decide to quit drinking/using, quit for a while, and then change our minds and pick up "that first one."

The personal experience this workbook draws upon, most of all, is your own decision to physically pick up that first drink or drug. Relapse is, indeed, a process. Yet many people begin the process without reaching the point of actually drinking/drugging. Something stops them. Of the people who do reach that fatal point, the overwhelming majority seem to have one of two kinds of thinking and sometimes both, as they decide to drink/use again.

Wishful Thinking

We'll call the first kind "wishful thinking." It shows up in thoughts like:

1. "I'll just have one."

2. "One won't hurt."

3. "This time will be different."

4. "I can handle it now."

5. "No one will know."

6. "I got in trouble with that, but not with this."

7. "But the doctor/dentist prescribed it!"

8. "I'll just get loaded once" (or for some limited time or occasion, i.e., "I'm on vacation").

9. Other (saying or implying "I will not lose control and no one will get hurt").

To the left of each example, write the number of times (from 1 to 5) you have said those words or something very close before picking up the first drink/drug of relapse. If more than five, write "5+." (If you have never quit drinking/drugging and then started again, simply ask yourself whether you have ever said these things to yourself as you picked up the first drink or drug of the day. How many times?)

(Note: if you have never experienced this kind of thinking as you picked up the first drink or drug, share with your counselor and group what you did tell yourself when making such decisions. Also, see if the second kind of thinking, described below, fits your experience.)

Share your total numbers with the others, and then run a total for the group. Share your feelings and/or sensations as you scored yourself and then as you learned the group scores. Each person share briefly what you think it means that so many people decide to drink/use again with almost the same thoughts.

(Note: if you are alone when answering these questions, write down what you would share if you were in a group. Some groups may choose to write out their answers first before sharing.)

The Expletive Response

The other sort of thinking that accompanies the first drink/drug (after a period of not drinking/using) is some sort of expletive—most commonly beginning with the letter F: "Who gives a -- --!" "To heck with it!" "Shine it!" Even a genteel "Oh well" or a weary "Whatever..." Regardless of the actual words, there is no claim of being in control. Just an expletive—a curse or some cluster of relatively meaningless words—and a load of apparently negative feelings. The curses, as you may know, can be pretty severe, so for reasons of taste we will refer to this as the "Dammit" relapse.

How many times have you started to drink/use with this sort of cursing or thinking? Circle a number below. (Again, if you have never returned to use after a period of not drinking/using, simply ask yourself if any kind of "Dammit" attitude has ever been part of your thinking as you picked up the first drink or drug of the day.)

0   1   2   3   4   5   More than five

Share your number with the others, and then run a total for the group. Share your feelings and/or sensations as you scored yourself and then as you learned the group scores. Each person share briefly what you think it means that so many people decide to drink/use again with this sort of thinking.

Lastly, each person share any change in feeling and/or physical sensation after sharing and discussing these thoughts that accompany the moment of physical relapse. Include any difference in group energy or energy in the workbook, which is entirely dedicated to using these thoughts to help you never "trip" again.

Summary

These two kinds of thinking are so common at moments of relapse that they may be seen as primary symptoms of addictive disease. Clearly, if you are not going to relapse again, you will have to prevent or defeat this kind of thinking in your own mind. "Wishful" and "Dammit" thinking give a human voice to the experience of taking that first drink/drug. And they give us somewhere to look for that invisible table that you want to stop tripping over. The decision to pick up the first drink or drug is usually a return to the thinking and decision-making that controlled us during active use. And to recover for good means to protect ourselves from our own thinking and decision making, especially when controlled by craving.

How would you rate your own willingness to look at your personal experience of deciding to pick up the first drink/drug? (Circle one.)

10. See no point and/or think it is a waste of time.

11. See no point, but curious where this is going.

12. See the point of focusing on this experience and trying to prevent it.

13. Eager to get at this and to try to understand and prevent it.

Share and discuss your answers. Notice similarities and differences among the group's answers.`

C. Two Biggest Barriers to "Getting It"

This workbook tries to help you realize things that enable you to do what is necessary to really work at staying clean and sober for good. One thing we have to do is see ourselves clearly, and that means realizing what it is that stands in our way.

1. *Shame:*

The mind/ego protects itself from seeing and admitting potentially shameful truths about the self. We are going to invite your mind to acknowledge shame every step of the way. We are going to invite you to share your experiences and feelings with others who have similar experiences and feelings. This is one of the most powerful ways to reduce shame.

Shame check: look back at how many times you have picked up that first drink/drug with wishful thinking or "Dammit" thinking. How reluctant would you be to share this truth with the important people in your life, assuming they do not have a drug or alcohol problem and they know that you do)?

1. Not at all   2. Slightly   3. Moderately   4. Extremely

How reluctant you are to share likely indicates how ashamed you may be, and how hard it will be to realize the very things that will help you never be shamed by this experience again.

Share your answers with a partner or group. Observe the similarities of experience and feelings, especially any sensations that arise in picturing yourself telling your loved ones what you think those times when you pick up the first drink. Notice even a slight change in how you feel about yourself after doing so. Do not be surprised if shame goes up before it goes down.

2. *Craving: the dark side of addiction:*

Addiction is a disease of desire, self-destructive desire that runs roughshod over healthy wants and needs, morals, and common sense. What the non-addict fails to see when judging the addict is a universal truth about craving, whether physical or mental.

All craving blinds the person who has it, whether we crave drugs, power, money, status, security, sex, parental love, or anything else to which the human brain may become attached. If we see a craving for what it is, we will take steps to control it. So the craving brain seems hardwired to block awareness of its true nature: "I can take it or leave it." "I can quit when I want to." "I just want it, I don't need it."

Wishful thinking puts a calm and rational cover over the powerful craving that motivates a person's decision at the moment of taking that first drink/drug. And in a "Dammit" moment, we are so focused on relief we don't even notice that craving has eliminated all other options. Craving blocks information that might lead to better decisions. And the deep-down knowledge that we are controlled by craving is a huge source of shame.

Rate how much you agree with the following statement:

"Craving has controlled my perceptions, thinking, and decisions."

1. Not at all   2. Slightly   3. Moderately   4. Totally

Here's how you can deal with craving in this group workbook. When processing each exercise, notice and share your own sensations. Look especially for anger and even rage, fear, or any sense of threat or defensiveness. The craving brain would like to hold on to its cravings, so these negative feelings can come up when you confront your cravings and try to uproot them.

Also, you are more likely to see craving at work in others than in yourself. If you observe craving in other people, try to share what you see compassionately and to be open to what others may see in you. The old saying about the pot calling the kettle black is true for the entire human race. But it is nowhere more true than in a room full of human beings struggling with addiction.

PART I: THE WISHFUL THINKING RELAPSE

The next four sections focus ONLY on relapse that begins with wishful thinking, thoughts like the ones listed below. (If you have never had such a relapse, you will be given other options for completing this part of the workbook.)

- "I'll just have one" or "One won't hurt."

- "This time will be different."

- "I can handle it now."

- "No one will know."

- "I got in trouble with that, but not with this."

- "But the doctor/dentist prescribed it!"

- "I'll just get loaded once" or for some limited time or occasion, i.e., "I'm on vacation."

- Other (saying or implying "I will not lose control and no one will get hurt").

(If you have NEVER had a period of being clean and sober which ended with you thinking these wishful thoughts, try to answer the questions in this section one of three ways:

1. Refer to any moment when you were reasonably clean/sober, even if you drank/drugged the day before. The important thing is that you decided to pick up that first drink/drug of the day with some idea of controlling your use. Some people do this daily, often after deciding to quit that morning! Or,

2. Imagine yourself relapsing with wishful thinking nine months from now, having failed to actively participate in recovery at all. Answer the questions in this section as if this has really happened. [Your "beginning" would be whenever you quit this time.] Or,

3. Answer the questions in this section for an actual moment of relapse when you used an expletive like "Dammit" as you decided to drink/drug again. Be sure to notice and discuss similarities and differences with people who relapsed through wishful thinking.

WISHFUL THINKING REALIZATION NUMBER ONE

Awareness of Suffering Scale

Picture yourself at the beginning of just one of your own actual times of being clean and sober, one that eventually ended with you telling yourself "I'll just have one," or any of the other thoughts above. (If you have not had this experience, use one of the three options above.) Something must have bothered you enough that you decided to quit drinking/using. This "bother" was some form of pain, suffering, or crisis, some sort of distressing sensation. When you were deciding to quit, you must have had some idea your suffering would go down or go away if you gave up alcohol/drugs.

On the scale below, your awareness of this pain, at the moment you decided to quit, falls at the 10 spot. This is your "personal worst," your maximum awareness of the pain drinking/drugging had brought you to at that point in your life. (Everyone's suffering is different, but we create a personal scale for you and your experience. The top of the scale marks your awareness of the worst pain that got you to quit.)

| 0 | 1 | 2 | 3 | 4 | 5 | 6 | 7 | 8 | 9 | ___**10**___ |

So, after feeling the pain that sits at the 10 spot, you quit. Now roll your "memory tape" forward through that period when you were staying clean and sober, right up to the moment that wishful thinking kicked in and you reached for the first drink/drug of your relapse. Try to remember how you felt at that very moment, just before taking that first drink/drug. How aware were you of the pain and suffering you felt before, which got you to quit? How strong was that awareness at the moment you decided to pick up again? You were a 10 in the beginning, when you quit. What were you at the very end, just before you picked up? (Circle a number on the same scale, above. And note: you are not measuring the amount of suffering but your awareness of the suffering that alcohol/drug use had caused you.)

Awareness of Suffering Scale

Beginning: 10 (maximum awareness of your suffering)	----- Clean and sober -----	End/Relapse: 1-10? (Awareness of that same suffering)

If you have had other periods of being clean and sober ending with wishful thinking, use the numbers below to chart your awareness. If the awareness of your suffering was 10 each time when you quit, what was it just before you started again?

| 0 | 1 | 2 | 3 | 4 | 5 | 6 | 7 | 8 | 9 | 10 |

| 0 | 1 | 2 | 3 | 4 | 5 | 6 | 7 | 8 | 9 | 10 |

| 0 | 1 | 2 | 3 | 4 | 5 | 6 | 7 | 8 | 9 | 10 |

Awareness of Suffering Over Time (your personal graph)

Beginning	Clean and sober	End/Relapse
10		10
9		9
8		8
7		7
6		6
5		5
4		4
3		3
2		2
1		1

What do you see?

Shame check: Can you feel shame, anxiety, and/or defensiveness going up?

How reluctant would you be to share this truth (about your drop in awareness before you started drinking/using again) with the important people in your life, especially if they have no alcohol/drug problem and know that you do?

      1. Not at all   2. Slightly   3. Moderately   4. Extremely

Rate how strongly you agree with this statement about your personal experience:

"When I decided to start drinking/drugging again (with wishful thinking), I seem to have forgotten both the pain that led me to quit and the fact that drinking/drugging caused it. For me, the process of relapse is at least partly a process of forgetting the suffering caused by drinking/using."

      1. Not at all   2. Slightly   3. Moderately   4. Totally

Now would be a good time to share your answers and the sensations you are experiencing with a partner and/or group. As before, notice similarities of experiences and feeling, as well as any changes you feel or observe after you have shared. Notice any change in group energy.

After sharing, rate your agreement with the following statements:

"If I do not find a way to remember the suffering caused by drinking/using, I will not be able to stay clean and/or sober."

      1. Not at all   2. Slightly   3. Moderately   4. Totally

"By myself, I seem unable to remember the suffering that motivated me to abstain."

    1. Not at all   2. Slightly   3. Moderately   4. Totally

"We are unable, at certain times, to bring into our consciousness with sufficient force the memory of the suffering and humiliation of even a week or a month ago."(*AA Big Book*, page 24.)

    1. Not at all   2. Slightly   3. Moderately   4. Totally

Rate your willingness to use peer meetings to help yourself and others remember why you are not taking even one drink/drug and what will happen if you forget:

    1. Not at all   2. Slightly   3. Moderately   4. Totally

Share your above ratings with the group and/or a partner. Be sure to give reasons for your ratings, based on your experience. When you are done, share your sensations as you did the exercise and as you discussed it. When everyone is done, do a quick share of any further sensations, including changes in group energy.

Homework (or in group):

In the space below, list any ways you have tried to remember the pain of active use while clean and sober in the past. How well did each tool or technique work? How long was it effective? What seems to happen to these tools over time?

_____

_____

_____

_____

_____

List the ways in which 12 Step programs provide ongoing reminders of what will happen if members forget their reasons to not take even one drink/drug.

_____

_____

_____

_____

_____

Share and discuss your answers. What do you "get" from this exercise? Does everyone in the group "get it"? If you have enough trust, give each other feedback on how much you see each other "getting it." You might use a 10-point scale to rate how much a person "gets it," backing it up with non-judgmental but specific feedback. (How can you tell whether someone "gets it" or not? What do you see or hear that tells you a person does not fully grasp the life-and-death necessity for maintaining awareness of suffering caused by use and how it affects the likelihood of relapse?)

Rate your agreement with the following:

"This exercise has increased my appreciation of how forgetting my own experience contributes to relapse."

1. Not at all   2. Slightly   3. Moderately   4. Totally

"This exercise has increased my appreciation of how 'working a program' contributes to remembering the things necessary to not take the first drink/drug."

1. Not at all   2. Slightly   3. Moderately   4. Totally

WISHFUL THINKING REALIZATION NUMBER TWO

Read the following list of "possible facts and conditions" that might be true for anyone picking up the first drink/drug with wishful thinking. (The list comes from hundreds of groups doing this exercise!) Put a check next to each one that was true for you the last time you did this. Count the check marks. (If you have never tried to stay clean and sober before, use that imaginary relapse nine months from now, a moment you started the day's drinking/using with wishful thinking, or any actual "Dammit" relapse you may have had.)

POSSIBLE FACTS AND CONDITIONS (AS I DECIDED TO PICK UP THE FIRST DRINK/DRUG WITH "WISHFUL THINKING")

1. I believed I could drink/drug and not suffer loss of control or painful consequences.

2. I believed I could drink/drug and not cause suffering for anyone else.

3. I was in denial and did not believe I am, in fact, an addict/alcoholic.

4. I believed I could use my "willpower" to control and enjoy my use of alcohol/drugs.

5. I knew I was an addict/alcoholic but thought I could "manage" it.

6. I was almost blind to the predictable consequences of use, and could not see clearly what was likely to happen.

7. In my mind, I was NOT deciding or planning to wind up back in treatment.

8. I was not planning to have to do a workbook like this.

9. (With hindsight, I see that) I actually wanted more than "just one," but I was not fully aware of it.

10. I was upset or troubled about some problem or situation in my life but was not aware of these feelings at that moment, nor was I "dealing with" the problem. (I had "put it out of my mind" and/or "stuffed" my feelings.)

11. I made little or no conscious connection between the stressful problem which was bothering me and my desire for alcohol and/or drugs. (In other words, I did not see that I was drinking to escape the problem I was not facing.)

12. I had pretty much forgotten the painful reasons I quit in the first place.

13. I was believing what I wanted to believe instead of basing my belief on the facts.

14. I was only dimly aware, if at all, of how great my craving was and how much it controlled me.

15. I thought I was going to have "fun," a "good time," a "party," etc.

16. I was elated, a bit euphoric, overexcited, almost like I had already had a mood-altering chemical.

17. I was bored.

18. I was complacent.

19. I was stressed or "on edge;" I thought a limited amount of the drug would take the edge off and give me some relief without getting out of hand.

20. I had some idea that I should not start, but the idea or feeling was too vague and/or dim to stop me.

21. Other (any fact or condition you did not see then that you do see now. Make a check mark for each one and add it to your total score).

Your score _____ (out of 21 or more.)

Read the items you have checked. Consider that each one is some form of unreality, describing a mind or attitude that is not based on the truth. That mind is making a decision, telling itself, "One won't hurt," "I can handle it," and the like. And each of the facts or conditions that you checked represents a step out of reality.

How many steps out of reality were you? _____

That is not the worst (most shameful or frightening) part. This is:

You hadn't consumed any drink or drugs at this point. At the moment you told yourself that it would be OK to take a drink/drug, what was your BAL (blood alcohol level)? _____

If you had taken a UA that precise moment of wishful thinking, before you'd taken the first drink/drug, what would your UA have shown? Positive or negative?

In other words, how many steps out of reality was your mind/brain before it even had a single molecule of drugs or alcohol in it?

It is our alcohol- and drug-free mind that picks up the first drink/drug. Dr. Jekyll makes the decision to create Mr. Hyde!

What are you feeling as you "get" this truth about any moment of deciding to pick up the first drink/drug? Check as many as apply. (If this is not new to you, check feelings you experienced the first time you "got it.")

Sick	Embarrassment
Numb	Stupid
Surprised	Shame

Nothing	Craving
Panic	Impulse to flee
Anxiety	Other_____ (specify)

Scan your body from head to toe as you take in the fact that we leave reality even *before* we take the first drink or drug. Write down any physical sensations that go with this experience.

If you were emotionally jarred by this exercise, you have suffered a "BFOTO" (blinding flash of the obvious, pronounced "buhfoto"). If you were not, hopefully you have suffered this in the past and already realize that your chemical-free mind leaves reality before you take the first drink/drug. If this BFOTO has never shaken you, you are more vulnerable to further relapse by wishful thinking.

Time to share with a partner and/or group. Listen to each other's feelings and reactions. Discuss what this realization means to you personally and how it may change your approach to recovery, if at all. Notice any change of connectedness and/or energy in the group when you share.

The reason this exercise can be so unnerving is an insidious form of denial called "disownership." I may admit "I" have a problem. It is just that the clean and sober "I" is assuming that the drunken/loaded "I" is *really* the problem. I believe I am okay as long as drunken/loaded "I" doesn't drink, which means that the regular me doesn't need to change; it is that maniac who shows up after I drink/drug who must change. Woops! I, clean and sober, have shifted the pea of ownership under the shell of assumption. And I don't even know I have done it!

This may take time to absorb. It can be buried and forgotten. But it can be nurtured and refreshed, even cherished. I can see my ownership of the wishful thinking decision, stop tripping over the table of disownership—the subtle assumption that my clean and sober self is not really the problem and does not have to change or work.

Rate how strongly you agree with the following statement:

"I see that I have been assuming that my problem lies in my drinking/drugging self, not my alcohol-free, drug-free self. But now I see that it's the clean and sober me who says 'I will just have one' (or "Dammit!") and picks up the first drink/drug of relapse."

1. Not at all   2. Slightly   3. Moderately   4. Totally

Once I see *who* takes the first drink, I also can see who must do the work to prevent or defeat my own wishful thinking. I can take ownership of my own relapse prevention and/or recovery. I can even take ownership of preserving my own ownership! I no longer "do it for her/him/them" because I see why *I* need to work to change and to maintain that change. I can stop feeling and acting like a "renter" of my abstinence and start actively taking care of it, like someone with a stake in how long it lasts. A real owner.

Now think about all the things you have read, heard, or experienced with 12 Step Recovery so far. If you are new to the program and/or to this realization, do not fret for a second if you can't think of much. Just ask yourself if you are open to the group answers and how they might apply to you. Write down ways that 12 Step Recovery helps us to face this fact about ourselves and the decision to pick up the first drink/drug. Specifically,

- How does the program take some of the sting out of this realization?

  _____

  _____

  _____

  _____

- How does the program turn this fact into a positive that works for us?

  _____

  _____

  _____

  _____

- Above all, how does the program preserve and deepen our experience and practice of ownership?

  _____

  _____

  _____

  _____

When everyone is ready, share your answers. Those who see how the program relates to this fundamental ownership of the decision to pick up the first drink/drug, try to share your actual experience with having this realization and how the program has helped you with it in the past, even if you eventually drank or used again.

Rate your agreement with the following statement:

"The BFOTO exercise has increased my awareness that it is my sober self who must change."

    1. Not at all   2. Slightly   3. Moderately   4. Totally

"The BFOTO exercise has increased my awareness that it is my sober self who must do the work of recovery and maintenance."

    1. Not at all   2. Slightly   3. Moderately   4. Totally

WISHFUL THINKING REALIZATION NUMBER THREE

Where there is a will, there is a way.
I can do anything I set my mind to.
Never surrender!
Quitters never prosper.
I can do anything anyone else can.
I have not yet begun to fight!
Damn the torpedoes—full speed ahead!
Live free or die!
When the going gets tough, the tough get going.
I did it my way!

Someone, possibly even you, seems to think you have failed to practice this sort of determination where alcohol/drugs are concerned. How reluctant would you be to share that failure with the important people in your life, assuming they do not have an alcohol or drug problem and they know that you do?

1. Not at all   2. Slightly   3. Moderately   4. Extremely

What is "willpower," and how does it relate to addiction, relapse, and wishful thinking? In plain English, "willpower" is stick-to-it-iveness, the ability to make a decision and hold to that decision without wavering. Addiction seems to involve the loss of this ability with regard to just two decisions, no matter how many others you may have carried through.

A. Loss of Stick-to-it-iveness <u>After</u> Taking the First Drink/Drug

How many times have you been clean and sober and told yourself you would have just one or only a couple, only to drink/drug longer than your initial intention and decision? This might include times you tried to limit how often you were going to drink/drug but ended up doing it far more frequently, and/or times you tried to limit yourself to certain kinds of drugs or alcohol but ended up using ones you said you wouldn't.

Never

1-5

6-10

11-20

more

(This does not mean you *never* have stuck to your decision to limit the amount and frequency of your drinking. It just means that your stick-to-it-iveness failed at times.)

Rate how much you agree with the following:

"Looking back at my actual experience, when I take the first drink/drug and tell myself I will limit my use, there seems to be no way of being 100% certain I will do as I said."

    1. Not at all   2. Slightly   3. Moderately   4. Totally

We do not just lose control of the quantity that we drink or drug. Some of the surest indicators that we are losing control are the unintended and unwanted consequences that result from using and would not have happened had we not been drinking or drugging.

List three to five painful experiences which occurred while drinking or using drugs, things that most likely would not have occurred had you not been under the influence and/or in drinking/drugging situations.

1. _____

2. _____

3. _____

4. _____

5. _____

Did you intend or plan for any of them to happen? Yes___ No___

When you decided to drink or drug on the days that these things happened, did you actually tell yourself you were going to control your use, not get out of hand, and stay out of trouble?

    Yes___ No___

If these painful experiences happened during a relapse, did you take the first drink/drug of that particular physical relapse with the idea that you would not get hurt and/or lose control?

    Yes___ No___

Rate how much you agree with the following:

"The only way to eliminate the risk of the loss of control that (sometimes) occurs when I drink/drug is to completely avoid alcohol/drugs."

    1. Not at all   2. Slightly   3. Moderately   4. Totally

Pick one of each of the following probabilities, the one that seems most true for you.

"If I take one drink or use one time, the likelihood of (sooner or later) losing control of both my use and the consequences would be:"

        1. Virtually none.   2. Slight   3. Moderate   4. Extremely high.

"If I forget my past lack of stick-to-it-iveness when I start drinking/drugging and the suffering that follows, the likelihood of my taking "that first one" would be:"

        1. Virtually none.   2. Slight   3. Moderate   4. Extremely high.

"If I do not stick to some sort of peer support meeting in the foreseeable future, the likelihood that I will forget about my lack of stick- to-it-ive-ness after taking the first drink would be:"

        1. Virtually none.   2. Slight   3. Moderate   4. Extremely high.

Share your answers about lack of "stick-to-it-iveness" (after the first drink/drug) and what you make of them with the group, including the sensations you experience as you think about the questions and the experience on which you base your answers.

After everyone has responded, share what it feels like to hear the answers of the group. Notice any change in group energy.

B. Loss of Stick-to-it-iveness <u>Before</u> Taking the First Drink/Drug

This one is scarier. Has this ever happened to you?

You decide to quit for good, realizing it really is the first drink/drug that leads to loss of control and suffering. You recognize that the only way to avoid the suffering and lost control is to avoid **any** drug or alcohol use. You do not drink or drug for weeks, months, or years. Yet one day, you change your mind and take the first drink/drug. Your stick-to-it-iveness did not stick! You "set your mind" and the darn thing came unset, apparently all by itself.

How many times have you decided to quit for good, only to start drinking/drugging again somewhere down the road?

0

1-3

4-10

more than 10

Rate how much you agree with the following statements:

"I have been unable, so far, to make up my mind to stay clean and sober and keep it made up. Like someone on a diet, the motivation and willpower I have in the beginning somehow fades in the end. I do not stick to my decision to quit drinking/drugging, not permanently."

1. Not at all   2. Slightly   3. Moderately   4. Totally

"As necessary and important as willpower may be, I am going to have to find something more than just my own willpower if I am to stick with my decision to stay clean and sober."

1. Not at all   2. Slightly   3. Moderately   4. Totally

Rate how willing you are to consistently seek out the support, energy and ideas of other people to keep your stick-to-it-iveness alive.

1. Not at all   2. Slightly   3. Moderately   4. Totally

Now think about all the things you have read, heard, or experienced with 12 Step Recovery so far. If you are new to the program and/or to this realization, do not fret for a second if you can't think of much. Just ask yourself if you are open to the group answers and to seeing how they might apply to you.

Write down ways that 12 Step Recovery helps us face our lack of stick-to-it-iveness before and after the decision to pick up the first drink/drug. Specifically:

- How does the program take some of the sting out of this realization?

_____

_____

- How does the program turn this fact into a positive that works for us?

  _____

  _____

- Above all, how does the program preserve and deepen our experience and practice of stick-to-it-iveness <u>before</u> we take the first drink/drug of physical relapse?

  _____

  _____

When everyone is ready, share your answers. Those who see how the program protects against the fatal lack of control, try to share your actual experience with having this realization and how the program has helped you with it, even some of the time.

Rate how much you agrees with the following statement:

"This section has increased my awareness that I do not control alcohol or drugs before use."

     1. Not at all   2. Slightly   3. Moderately   4. Totally

"This section has increased my awareness that I do not control alcohol or drugs after I start."

     1. Not at all   2. Slightly   3. Moderately   4. Totally

WISHFUL THINKING REALIZATION NUMBER FOUR

Rate how much you agree with the following:

"When I decide to drink/drug based on any form of wishful thinking, I am making a life-and-death decision based on a belief that is not true for me, may never have been true, or has not been true in a long time. Furthermore, every painful thing that has already happened as a result of my drinking/drugging, regardless of what I tell myself when I start, demonstrates that my wishful belief is not true. I hurt myself and I hurt others:"

1. Not at all   2. Slightly   3. Moderately   4. Totally

Now would be a good time to share with a partner and/or group. Include any objections and/or feelings about the above statement, as well as physical sensations you had while you were reading and answering the question. Notice similarities and differences in the group, as well as how the connectedness of the group is affected by this sharing.

Addict thinking versus schizophrenic thinking

A. Richard, a schizophrenic, forms the belief that he is a "bird."

B. Based on this belief, he decides to "fly" out the window.

C. He suffers the consequences of his action—a broken neck and death.

A. An alcoholic/addict forms the belief that "one won't hurt," "I wasn't that bad," "I can handle it now," or the like.

B. Based on this belief, s/he decides to have "just one."

C. S/he suffers the consequences of losing control—painful and unexpected events, often dying younger than Richard did.

Share your first reactions with a partner and/or group. Focus on the first emotion, sensation, reaction, or thought that occurred when you read this comparison. Then take turns stepping back and looking at similarities and differences between the doomed schizophrenic and an alcoholic/addict believing his or her own wishful thinking as she or he picks up the first drink or drug. Notice any variation in the group's connectedness as you share about this. Notice yourself and others resisting and/or digesting this. Discuss what you think happens to people who do not "get" this.

Rate your agreement with the following statement:

"My chemical-free mind makes irrational decisions where alcohol/drugs are concerned. My own 'reality testing' is not to be trusted."

    1. Not at all   2. Slightly   3. Moderately   4. Totally

Rate how willing you are to share your actual thoughts with others, not waiting to be asked, in order to check your own tendency for "stinking thinking" and prevent relapse.

    1. Not at all   2. Slightly   3. Moderately   4. Totally

Again, think about all the things you have read, heard, or experienced with 12 Step Recovery so far. If you are new to the program and/or to this realization, do not fret for a second if you can't think of much. Just ask yourself if you are open to the group's answers and to seeing how they might apply to you. Specifically,

- Write down ways that 12 Step Recovery helps us to face our insanity. How does the program take some of the sting out of this realization?

  _____

  _____

  _____

  _____

- How does the program turn this fact into a positive that works for us?

  _____

  _____

  _____

- Above all, how does the program preserve and deepen our experience and practice of sanity before we take the first drink/drug of physical relapse?

  _____

  _____

  _____

  _____

When everyone is ready, share your answers. Those who see how the program protects against insanity, try to share your actual experience with having this realization about yourself and how the program has helped you with it, even if you drank/drugged again later.

Rate how much you agree with the following statement:

"Wishful Thinking Realization Number Four has increased my understanding and acceptance that wishful thinking is in fact a form of insanity, and that I must work to restore my sanity and to maintain it."

1. Not at all   2. Slightly   3. Moderately   4. Totally

Self-Assessment

Review your work on the four realizations about wishful thinking. Then complete the following ratings and/or sentences.

Rate how much you agree with the following statement:

"In doing these four sections on wishful thinking, I feel that my eyes have been opened about what is really going on when I tell myself I can drink/drug without losing control or suffering."

1. Not at all   2. Slightly   3. Moderately   4. Totally

The realization that felt the most emotional was (circle one):

1. That I actually forget my reasons to not pick up the first drink/drug.

2. That it is my clean and sober mind that decides to pick up the first drink/drug.

3. That I lack stick-to-it-iveness, both before and after the first drink/drug.

4. That my wishful thinking is irrational and is a form of insanity.

The realization that most changed how I think about addiction and recovery was (circle one):

1. That I actually forget my reasons to abstain.

2. That it is my clean and sober mind decides to pick up the first drink/drug

3. That I lack stick-to-it-iveness, both before and after the first drink/drug.

4. That my wishful thinking is irrational and is a form of insanity.

As a result of what I now "get" about my own wishful thinking, I am more likely to (circle all that apply):

1. Attend peer support meetings, and aftercare if it is available.

2. Attend 12 Step meetings.

3. Get a sponsor.

4. Attend 90 meetings in 90 days.

5. Remain clean and sober.

6. Continue individual counseling or psychotherapy.

7. Be working at my recovery one year from now, including peer support groups.

8. Be working at my recovery three years from now, including peer support groups.

9. Be working at my recovery ten years from now, including peer support groups.

10. Really work to find some form of spiritual experience or transformation.

11. Other:

Share and discuss your answers, focusing on what you "got" and what seemed to help you do so.

ANONYMOUS MAINTENANCE PLAN SCALE: AFTER PART I

This page is an anonymous survey, designed to collect results for the whole group. It tries to measure how much difference the workbook/group is making overall. You were asked to choose one "plan" before you started the workbook. You are being asked to choose one again now and you will be again after Part II. An honest answer on this scale will make the workbook better for others over the long haul. Other questions inside the workbook give you a chance to assess and discuss how it is working for you and your group.

Do not put your name on this page---it is meant to be cut out and handed in.

Your counselor may ask you all to put a date or some other mark on the page so s/he knows which group s/he is recording. S/he will calculate only the average numbers for your group.

Below are five possible ways to maintain your own recovery after completing this workbook and any program of which it is a part. Please, circle the one that most closely describes what you are likely to do after you finish the workbook and the program, even if the description is not perfect.

The closest description of my plan to stay clean and sober after completing this program

1. None. I plan to return to the use of alcohol and/or drugs.

2. Just stay away from drugs and alcohol, using my willpower.

3. Start or resume at least one activity, such as exercise, a nutritional program, a new hobby, or even more time working, to "stay busy" or "keep me going" (without returning to alcohol/drugs). I will not involve myself with any sort of "mutual help" group.

4. Whether I also do parts of number 3 or not, I will attend some sort of "mutual help" meetings until I feel "out of the woods" and able to stay off drugs/alcohol on my own. Or I might participate in some form of psychotherapy until I think I am ready to stay clean and sober on my own. Or I will stay clean and sober solely through my religion, without participation in groups or activities specifically for recovering alcoholic/addicts.

5. Even if I also do some of the above, I will join a 12 Step Program, get a sponsor, work the steps, and attend meetings. If I have already started this, I will continue under the guidance of my sponsor.

CUT HERE

PART II: THE EXPLETIVE ("DAMMIT!") RELAPSE

The four sections of Part II are focused entirely on what we can learn from the "Dammit" or expletive relapse.   (If you have never had such a relapse, you will be given other options for completing this part of the workbook.)

In a published exercise called "Expletive Deleted," thousands of patients and workshop participants consistently provided the following "translations" of what they really meant when they said "Dammit" (or the less polite version) when they relapsed.

1. I don't care!   _____   _____

2. I give up/I quit!   _____   _____

3. What's the use?   _____   _____

4. Damn you (or me)!   _____   _____

5. I've had it!   _____   _____

If you have done this, picture the last time when you stayed clean and sober for a while, but then decided to drink or use again with "Dammit!" (or some other curse or expletive) in your mind. Circle the translation above that you identify with the most, the one that best fits your meaning or attitude that time. (If you don't identify strongly with one of the examples, write in your own translation.) How many other times in your life has this attitude accompanied the first drink/drug of physical relapse? Write the total number on the first line to the right of the one you selected.

(Note: If you have NEVER been clean and sober and then started to drink/use again with "Dammit" or some other expletive, try to answer the questions in this section one of three ways:

(Circle the option that you are going to use.)

1. First option: Use any moment when you were reasonably clean/sober, even if you drank/ drugged the day before. The important thing is that you decided to pick up that first drink/drug of the day with an expletive or curse of some kind. Or,

2. Second Option: Answer the questions in Part II for an actual moment when you had been clean and sober, made your decision to drink/drug again with "wishful thinking" in your mind. This option will *only* be useful if you can now see that you were seeking relief from any sort of distress, however mild. You may or may not have been aware of it at the time. Based on your attitude about this upset rather than your actual words, pick the best translation(s) for you from the list above. Or,

3. Third Option: Imagine yourself relapsing that way (with expletive thinking) nine months from now, having failed to actively participate in recovery at all. Perhaps you can imagine something that might get you upset enough to curse or use some other expletive and relapse. Then answer the questions in this section as if this has really happened. [Your "beginning" will be when you began your current period of not drinking or drugging.]

Draw a square around the "translation" you identify with second most. You may have meant it less frequently when you picked up the first drink/drug. Or it may have been part of your meaning, but not something you felt as strongly as the one you circled. Even if you are using one of the three "options," how many times have you meant this when picking up the first drink or drug? Write that number on the second line to the right of the list above.

Check any *other* translation you identify with to any degree. Next to it, write the number of times you have meant this as you picked up the first drink/drug of physical relapse.

Shame check: How reluctant would you be to share your translations—that this is what you actually think and mean when you are deciding to pick up that first drink/drug? Especially with the important people in your life, assuming they do not have an alcohol or drug problem and they know that you do?

1. Not at all   2. Slightly   3. Moderately   4. Extremely

Share and discuss your answers with a partner and/or group, as well as the emotions and physical sensations you felt while answering. What do each of you make of this, your translations and any reluctance you feel to share them? Notice how your shame and the connectedness and energy of the group fluctuate with the sharing.

EXPLETIVE ("DAMMIT") RELAPSE REALIZATION NUMBER ONE

The translations are rewritten again below. It may or may not be obvious to you that there is a pattern here, something all of these translations have in common. But there is, and it reveals one of the tables we all trip over when we say "Dammit!" and relapse. This exercise gives you a way, first as an individual, then as a group, to identify that table and to "get it," to see what is necessary to avoid tripping again.

Each translation has been left open-ended. Starting with the one you identify with the most, try to finish each of the sentences with something real you have or would have said that about.

I don't care about .... !

I give up or I quit trying to .... !

What's the use of.. !

Damn you/me for .... !

I've had it with .... !

(Other)_____because.. !

Now, look for something that all of your examples have in common. (As you commit to understanding yourself, keep in mind: It is more important to struggle for an answer than to be the one who finds it. Once you have struggled on your own, it will be far easier to recognize an answer offered by someone else.) Write down anything that occurs to you:

Next, compare your answers to those of at least one other person and then the whole group. What is it that all of these experiences have in common? The task now is for the whole group to come up with at least one general category or phrase to complete all of the sentences in the same way.

You are looking for something that these different translations, by different people in different circumstances, all have in common. You are looking for a table that has tripped each of you, every time you said "Dammit" and picked up the first drink/drug. Tables come in many shapes, sizes, colors and materials, but they all have enough in common to be called "tables." Take your time. Try to be thorough yet simple. Struggling with this task is to be expected.

Your facilitator will let the group know if you come up with a single way of finishing the sentences that works (for the work that follows). Other answers are not necessarily "wrong." In fact, they are usually accurate and based on experience. But they may be too general or too specific to help bring the "table" into focus.

After you have all done your best, share with each other what it felt like to try this exercise. How frustrating, silly, or embarrassing was it?

When everyone has shared about the above questions, take a look at yet another version of the translations:

1. I don't care about people, places, and things!

2. I give up or I quit trying to get what I want from people, places, and things!

3. What's the use trying to get what I want from people, places, and things?

4. "Damn" people, places, and things (even myself)!

5. I've had it with people, places, and things!

6. (Other) _____ because of people, places, and things!

If the original translations expressed what "Dammit!" really meant, these translations tell us what the "it" part of that was. "Damn" what? The people, places, and things in our lives. We say "Dammit" to those things and then we trip on that table yet again.

So what do we have to do instead of saying our favorite curse and tripping? What are some specific verbs or phrases that express what we can *do* regarding the people, places, and things in our lives? Write your answers in the space below.

Now share your answers with a partner and/or group. What words did you all come up with?

Many groups come up with phrases like "deal with it," "handle stress," or even "cope."

Rate your agreement with the following statement:

"When I picked up the first drink/drug with the thought, 'Dammit,' I had lost the willingness and/or ability to cope in any other way."

      1. Not at all   2. Slightly   3. Moderately   4. Totally

"Neurotics" have nervous breakdowns. "Schizophrenics" have psychotic breaks. Alcoholics and addicts experience a breakdown of the willingness and/or ability to cope. We "snap." And we usually spit out a curse like "Dammit!" when we do. But the four-letter expletive must be replaced by the four-letter task C-O-P-E. (This, in fact, requires another four letter word: W-O-R-K!)

How surprised are you to see that the "Dammit!" relapse is a breakdown of the willingness and/or ability to cope?

      1. Not at all   2. Slightly   3. Moderately   4. Totally

Whether you are surprised or not, how would you rate your shame about this fact? How eager would you be to share this truth—that your relapse resulted from a failure to cope—with the important people in your life, assuming they do not have an alcohol or drug problem and they know that you do?

1. Not at all   2. Slightly   3. Moderately   4. Extremely

Share your answers with a partner/group. Notice the similarities in their reactions (don't worry about differences). Notice how you feel about yourselves and each other after you have shared. Share that!

We actually have two names for the table we trip on: "coping" and "people, places, and things." But it is not the person place or thing itself that we find so intolerable. It is the simple fact that, in some way that is important to us, the person, place, or thing, is not how we *want* it to be! The name for this is "frustration."

Rate your agreement with the following:

"I say 'Dammit' or some other expletive and pick up the first drink/drug when I am frustrated."

1. Not at all   2. Slightly   3. Moderately   4. Totally

Rate how motivated you are to learn healthier, wiser, and more effective ways to cope with frustration (instead of saying "Dammit!" and picking up that first drink/drug).

1. Not at all   2. Slightly   3. Moderately   4. Totally

Rate how motivated you are to do something on a continuing basis to renew and maintain your willingness to work at coping with your life.

1. Not at all   2. Slightly   3. Moderately   4. Totally

Frustration: a closer look

Frustration is something that happens when either (1) we don't get what we want or (2) we do get what we don't want. Truth be told, this happens all day long, and we do not drink/drug over it.

Look back at your last "Dammit" relapse. Spell out as specifically as you can what you wanted versus what you were getting at the moment you said "Dammit." (And here we are not talking about wanting the "relief" of taking the drink/drug. You wanted relief because you were frustrated, and you were frustrated because something didn't turn out the way you wanted. So what was it you wanted so badly?)

The person, place, thing, or situation that had me so upset that I said "Dammit!" and took the first drink/drug was:

_____

_____

_____

_____

Rate how much you agree with the following statements about the frustration you have just listed:

"I did not merely *want* what I wanted. I *expected* it."

      1. Not at all   2. Slightly   3. Moderately   4. Totally

"The more I expect something, the more I demand it. The more I demand it, the more upset I become when my expectation is not met."

      1. Not at all   2. Slightly   3. Moderately   4. Totally

"In order for me not to say 'Dammit!' and drink/use when my expectations are not met, I must find ways to lower my expectations of people, places, things and situations."

      1. Not at all   2. Slightly   3. Moderately   4. Totally

"I did not merely *want* what I wanted. I *resented* that I was not getting it."

      1. Not at all   2. Slightly   3. Moderately   4. Totally

(In actual fact, it is unlikely that anyone has EVER, in the history of addiction and the human race, said "Dammit" and relapsed without resentment. Buddhists say that resenting your enemy is like swallowing rat poison and thinking it will kill the rat. The *AA Big Book* observes that "Resentment is the number one offender—it destroys more alcoholics than anything else.")

"If I do not learn how to prevent and/or relieve my own resentments, I am far more likely to continue having 'Dammit' relapses."

      1. Not at all   2. Slightly   3. Moderately   4. Totally

"I did not merely *want* what I wanted, I *craved* it."

       1. Not at all   2. Slightly   3. Moderately   4. Totally

"If expectation, resentment, and craving were eliminated from this situation, the craving for relief by alcohol/drugs would have been greatly reduced, if not eliminated."

       1. Not at all   2. Slightly   3. Moderately   4. Totally

"Frustration of my craving for something non-chemical—a person, place, or thing that I can't get and over which I have no control— can trigger my craving for alcohol/drugs, which I can always get, even if I can't control their use."

       1. Not at all   2. Slightly   3. Moderately   4. Totally

"I now see that what I wanted when I said 'Dammit!' and took the first drink/drug was more of a want than a need. I could have lived without it, even without the relief of drugs or alcohol."

       1. Not at all   2. Slightly   3. Moderately   4. Totally

"My ability to avoid future relapses of the 'Dammit' variety will very much depend on my ability to tell the difference between a want and a need, especially when I am upset."

       1. Not at all   2. Slightly   3. Moderately   4. Totally

"My own answers to these questions increase my understanding of the need to reduce expectations, resentments, and cravings if I am to avoid saying 'Dammit' and having a relapse."

       1. Not at all   2. Slightly   3. Moderately   4. Totally

Distress/Suffering

The questions above have asked you to put a laser focus on your own experience(s) of saying "Dammit!" and picking up the first drink/drug. Now we will look at the general role that stress and emotion play in our lives.

Without actually reliving (unless it helps!) your most recent "Dammit" relapse, look back at the emotional distress—the painful sensations in your body at that time—and the people, places, things, or situations which seemed to give rise to that suffering.

How does your distress at the moment of relapse compare to each of the OTHER times you used alcohol/drugs?

       1. Not at all   2. Slightly   3. Moderately   4. Totally

Were these similar sensations and circumstances OFTEN involved in your active use? Did you drink/drug to escape, avoid, or numb such sensations?

       1. Not at all   2. Slightly   3. Moderately   4. Totally

If you can identify when you "crossed the line" into active addiction, were you suffering from these sensations and circumstances at that time?

       1. Not at all   2. Slightly   3. Moderately   4. Totally 5. N.A.

With hindsight, can you see any of these sensations and circumstances playing a part in any wishful thinking relapses you may have had? Did you tell yourself, perhaps, you would have "just one" when in fact you were suffering from the same sort of sensations that you tried to relieve when you said "Dammit" and relapsed?

       1. Not at all   2. Slightly   3. Moderately   4. Totally

What I get from answering these questions comparing my sensations and circumstances throughout my drinking/drugging life is (circle one):

1. Nothing.

2. Some sense of connection between the different experiences.

3. A pretty clear pattern.

4. Wow! This is what I have to fix!

Write down briefly what you did or did not "get."

_____

_____

_____

_____

Time to share! Again, think about all the things you have read, heard, or experienced with 12 Step Recovery so far. If you are new to the program and/or to this realization, do not fret for a second if you can't think of much. Just ask yourself if you are open to the group's answers and how they might apply to you.

Write down ways that 12 Step Recovery helps us cope with frustration, including resentment, expectation, and wants that feel like needs or cravings. Specifically:

- How does the program take some of the sting out of the realization that our apparent cravings for people, places, things, or situations to be a certain way may trigger cravings for the relief of the "Dammit" relapse?

_____

_____

_____

_____

- How does the program help us see the difference between a want and a need, especially when we are becoming upset?

_____

_____

_____

_____

- Above all, how does the program help us to live inside our own skin in a life of constant frustration, without developing sensations that seem so intolerable that only drinking or drugging will relieve them?

_____

_____

_____

_____

When everyone is ready, share your answers. Those who see how the program protects against frustration, try to share your actual experience with having this realization about yourself and how the program has helped you with it, even if you drank/drugged again later.

Rate your agreement with the following statement:

"Expletive ('Dammit') Relapse Realization Number One has increased my understanding and acceptance that I must strengthen and maintain my ability and willingness to cope with frustration if I am to resist saying 'Dammit' and having a relapse."

1. Not at all   2. Slightly   3. Moderately   4. Totally

The Spiritual Significance of "Dammit"

Do you see saying an expletive when frustrated as a spiritual problem? How different is it from "taking the Lord's name in vain" when frustrated? Reflect on this a bit.

One way to think about it is to imagine a spiritual person—Jesus, Buddha, St. Francis, Mother Teresa, or even a 12 Step member, any spiritual person who seems to have real peace. Would they say "Dammit" (or worse!) when frustrated by people, places, things, or situations and seek chemical or material comfort? What might they do instead? How does their spirituality help them to cope? Write two or three sentences expressing your thoughts on this. Share with a partner and/or group.

_____

_____

_____

Having shared this, consider another translation of "Dammit" (or any other expletive preceding the first drink/drug of relapse):

"If life does not give me what I want, or gives me too much of what I don't want, I am out of here! And I know just how to leave!"

How much does this translation fit your attitude when you said "Dammit" and picked up the first drink/drug?

1. Not at all   2. Slightly   3. Moderately   4. Totally

Shame check: Rate your level of shame upon recognizing this attitude in yourself, without any alcohol or drug yet in your brain. How reluctant would you be to share this truth about your attitude when you relapse ("I am out of here!") with the important people in your life, assuming they do not have an alcohol or drug problem and they know that you do?

1. Not at all   2. Slightly   3. Moderately   4. Extremely

Whether we acknowledge it or not, the "Dammit" before taking the first drink/drug of relapse says to reality, "My way or the highway."

Read pages 60 (starting with "The first requirement…") to 62 (ending with "We must, or it kills us!) of *Alcoholics Anonymous*. To what degree do you identify with the statement "the alcoholic (addict) is an extreme example of self-will run riot"?

1. Not at all   2. Slightly   3. Moderately   4. Totally

If not, how are you different?

If so, how much do you agree that you need to "surrender" this demanding attitude, whether you believe in any specific "God" or not?

1. Not at all   2. Slightly   3. Moderately   4. Totally

How open are you to some sort of spirituality that:

- ✓ accepts reality instead of resisting it?

- ✓ lives in the present, not the past or future?

- ✓ feels connected to life and others?

- ✓ develops a sense of purpose?

1. Not at all   2. Slightly   3. Moderately   4. Totally

Share and discuss!

EXPLETIVE ("DAMMIT") RELAPSE REALIZATION NUMBER TWO

How strongly would you agree that the following "translation" fits your attitude and action at the moment of your "Dammit" relapse(s) or whatever option (1, 2, or 3) you are using for Part II?

"I quit or give up. I am throwing in the towel (on being clean and sober and/or on whatever I may be upset about.)"

1. Not at all   2. Slightly   3. Moderately   4. Totally

How many times have you had this experience?

Never

Once

Two or three times

Four or five times

More than five times

Shame check: How reluctant would you be to share this truth—that some of your relapses were about giving up or quitting—with the important people in your life, assuming they do not have an alcohol or drug problem and they know that you do?

1. Not at all   2. Slightly   3. Moderately   4. Extremely

Rate how strongly you have believed yourself, up until now, to be a "quitter."

1. Not at all   2. Slightly   3. Moderately   4. Totally

Rate how much you agree with the following:

"My ideals and/or values make it unacceptable to quit. If saying 'Dammit' and picking up the first drink/drug is quitting, I will go to great lengths to make sure that never happens again."

1. Not at all   2. Slightly   3. Moderately   4. Totally

Share with a partner/group your feelings, sensations, and thoughts in answering these questions. Notice how much others do or do not identify with "quitting." Notice how their thoughts and feelings compare to yours.

Even if you identify only somewhat with the above description, rate how much you agree with the following:

> "My clean and sober self is going to have to rely on someone/something other than my own mind or will if I am to resist becoming so overwhelmed and frustrated that a drink/drug appears to be the solution. Otherwise, sooner or later, I will give up, say 'Dammit,' (or the like), and take that first drink/drug."

1. Not at all   2. Slightly   3. Moderately   4. Totally

Rate how much you agree with the following:

> "If I am not to have another 'Dammit' relapse, I must find ways to not give up when things 'go wrong,' when my wants, needs, or rights seem blocked."

1. Not at all   2. Slightly   3. Moderately   4. Totally

Share with a partner/group your feelings and thoughts in answering these questions. Notice how their thoughts and feelings compare to yours. Notice any change in the energy or connectedness of the group.

Again, think about all the things you have read, heard, or experienced with 12 Step Recovery so far. If you are new to the program and/or to this realization, do not fret for a second if you can't think of much. Just ask yourself if you are open to the group's answers and how they might apply to you.

Write down ways that 12 Step Recovery helps us either (1) keep going when we're frustrated or (2) stop trying when something seems impossible—*without* going back to alcohol/drugs. Specifically:

- How does the program help us continue in the effort to remain sober even when some of our other efforts seem futile?

  _____

  _____

  _____

  _____

- What tools and/or principles do you already know about? Share any that have helped you stay sober in the past, even if you did eventually drink/drug again.

  _____

  _____

  _____

  _____

- When you experience sensations which make it seem like quitting is the only thing that will give you relief, what does 12 Step Recovery suggest you do about those sensations? What sensations do they promise if you do what they suggest? Does anyone in the group have experience of that truth, even if you drank/drugged again later? Share and discuss.

_____

_____

_____

_____

Rate how much you agree with the following statements:

"Answering these questions about how the 'Dammit!' relapse is an act of quitting has increased my understanding of what I must change in order to prevent such a relapse in the future."

     1. Not at all   2. Slightly   3. Moderately   4. Totally

One thing I must never quit is whatever I do to protect myself from throwing in the towel with a "Dammit" relapse!

     1. Not at all   2. Slightly   3. Moderately   4. Totally

EXPLETIVE ("DAMMIT") RELAPSE REALIZATION NUMBER THREE

Picture yourself a few days before your last relapse. To what degree would you have agreed with the following statement that day?

"I see myself as a caring individual."

    1. Not at all   2. Slightly   3. Moderately   4. Totally

In over fifteen years of doing an exercise called "Expletive Deleted" (referred to above, on p.29), by far the most consistent group translation of "Dammit" (or you know what!) has been "I don't care." This "uncaring" seems to break down two different ways:

C. <u>Not caring about what has ALREADY happened</u>. When we say "Dammit" about what has already happened, we deny caring about the people, places, things, or situations that have upset us.

D. <u>Not caring about what WILL happen</u>. When we say "Dammit" about what will happen after we drink/drug, we deny caring about the consequences of our actions, the price we may have to pay.

Let us start with A, not caring about what has already happened, typically involving the person place or thing that was frustrating. When you have said "Dammit" or the like and picked up the first drink/drug of relapse, how much was "I don't care about whatever has already happened" your attitude?

    1. Not at all   2. Slightly   3. Moderately   4. Totally

At the moment you said "Dammit" and picked up the first drink/drug, how upset or stressed were you? (Circle one. 10 is the most upset you have ever been.)

    1   2   3   4   5   6   7   8   9   10

If you were even somewhat upset, how much did you care about whatever it was that was upsetting you? (We do not get upset about something we do not care about! Circle one. 10 is the most you have ever cared about anything.)

    1   2   3   4   5   6   7   8   9   10

Do your answers to the above three questions reveal any contradiction between your meaning "I don't care" at the moment of a "Dammit!" relapse and the upset that tells us you really did care? Yes____ No____

If you answered "yes" above, write down how you feel about saying "Dammit"/"I don't care!" when you apparently cared so much about something that a drink/drug seemed like the necessary, justifiable relief?

_____

_____

_____

Shame Check: If you did answer "yes" above, how reluctant would you be to share this truth—that you said "I don't care!" in a moment when you actually cared a lot, leading to a relapse—with the important people in your life, assuming they do not have an alcohol or drug problem and they know that you do?

1. Not at all   2. Slightly   3. Moderately   4. Extremely   5. N.A.

Now share your feelings with a partner and/or the group, especially if you said, "Dammit"/"I don't care" when you apparently cared so much. Only after sharing your feelings about this contradiction, step back and discuss with each other, what you think it means.

Without reliving them too much, step back and look at the sensations of your distress, everything you felt inside your body at the moment you said "Dammit" and relapsed. You may also list any thoughts of distress or impulses, but be sure to spell out what you felt in your body.

_____

_____

_____

Looking at the sensations of relief you may have gotten from alcohol/drugs after saying "Dammit," how effective was this in stopping the painful sensations? (Circle one. On this scale, 1 is equal to 10% effective, and 10 is equal to 100% effective—i.e., it made all of the pain go away.)

1   2   3   4   5   6   7   8   9   10

How long was it until the painful sensations came back? _____

Going back to the moment of relapse, how much of the painful sensations (which led you to say "Dammit") would have been relieved if instead you had accepted things as they were (i.e., taken no for an answer, let go, surrendered, detached, or just stopped banging your head against a stone wall? 10 is 100% relief and 1 is 10% relief or less.

1   2   3   4   5   6   7   8   9   10

In your estimation, what percentage of the suffering and misery in your life has resulted from the unwillingness and/or inability to take no for an answer, to accept things as they are? Circle one. 10 is 100% and 1 is 10% or less.

1   2   3   4   5   6   7   8   9   10

List five things you care about, starting with the most important:

1. _____

2. _____

3. _____

4. _____

5. _____

Next to each, write down what will happen (or already has!) to it if you (continue to) say "Dammit" and relapse. How long before you will lose each thing (or how long since you already have)? Write down the sensations you will experience if/when you lose each thing, or when you actually did. Finally, write down and share the sensations you experience when you answer these questions.

_____

_____

_____

Remembering all of what is really important to us in life when we are upset is called "perspective." Rate your track record at maintaining perspective when agitated or upset about specific people, places, things, or situations. Be as honest as possible. (Circle a number, where 1 is equal to "dismal" and 10 is equal to "solid as a rock.")

1   2   3   4   5   6   7   8   9   10

Again, think about all the things you have read, heard, or experienced with 12 Step Recovery so far. If you are new to the program and/or to this realization, do not fret for a second if you can't think of much. Just ask yourself if you are open to the group's answers and to seeing if they apply to you. Write down ways that 12 Step Recovery helps us to hang on to our perspective, to remember what is really most important to us, even when some particular person, place, or thing has us painfully frustrated? Specifically:

- How does the program help us remember what else is important when the frustration of one or more important things fills mind and body with sensations that seem so painful the only way to relieve them is to say "Dammit" and take the first drink/drug?

  _____

  _____

  _____

  _____

- What tools and/or principles do you already know about? Share any that have helped you keep your perspective and not say "Dammit" in the past, even if you did eventually drink/drug again.

  _____

  _____

  _____

  _____

- When you experience sensations which make it seem like it is just too painful to continue caring, let alone remain sober and clean, what does 12 Step Recovery suggest you do about those sensations? What sensations do they promise if you do what they suggest?

  _____

  _____

  _____

  _____

When everyone is ready, share your answers. Those who see how the program protects against loss of perspective, try to share your actual experience with successfully practicing this, even if you eventually drank/drugged again.

Rate how much you agree with the following:

Part A of Realization Number Three—not caring about what has ALREADY happened—has increased my understanding of the need to remember what is most important to me when I am upset, if I am not to say "Dammit" and take that first drink/ drug ever again.

1. Not at all   2. Slightly   3. Moderately   4. Totally

B. Not Caring about What WILL Happen (after the first drink/drug)

Look at a moment you said "Dammit" and picked up the first drink/drug. How much, in that moment, were you really saying, "I don't care about the consequences of starting to drink/use again!"

1. Not at all   2. Slightly   3. Moderately   4. Totally

Even if you do not identify with the translation above, rate how much you agree with the following:

"At the moment I said 'Dammit' and picked up that first drink/drug, I was not thinking about the consequences and how painful they would be."

1. Not at all   2. Slightly   3. Moderately   4. Totally

Circle the check next to the areas in which you experienced consequences that would not have occurred if you had not taken that first drink/drug.

✓ family/relationships

✓ work, professional, school

✓ medical

✓ legal

✓ financial

✓ self-worth

✓ other

Did/do you suffer physically or emotionally because of these consequences of returning to use?

Yes ___ No___

If you answer "yes" above, how much of your suffering would have occurred if you did not, in fact, care about these very consequences?

1. None   2. Some   3. Most   4. All   5. N.A.

If you identify with meaning (at the moment of saying "Dammit")you did *not* care about the consequences of returning to use, and yet you suffered from the actual consequences, what do you make of that? What sensations do you experience when you think about this?

_____

_____

_____

_____

If you simply *did not think about* the consequences of returning to use, and then you suffered significantly from the consequences (which you so clearly cared about), what do you make of that? What sensations do you experience when you think about this?

_____

_____

_____

_____

Shame check: How reluctant would you be to share this truth—that you either denied caring about the consequences of relapse or didn't think about them at all (whichever is true for you)—with the important people in your life, assuming they do not have an alcohol or drug problem and they know that you do?

1. Not at all   2. Slightly   3. Moderately   4. Extremely

Share with partner and/or will group. Notice similarities. Notice any change in your feelings as you share. Share how it feels to share with each other.

Without reliving it too much, consider the pain you were in at the moment you said "Dammit," the pain that led you either to deny or overlook the consequences of taking the first drink/drug. If you had not sought the relief of alcohol/drugs, how long do you think it would have taken for the pain you felt in that moment to become at least tolerable? (Make your best guess. Pick one measurement below and give it a number.)

_____ minutes _____ hours _____ days _____ weeks _____ months _____years

Comparing the pain at that moment of saying "Dammit" with the pain of the consequences that resulted from relapsing, pick the best description for you:

1. The pain at that moment was far worse than anything that resulted from the relapse.

2. The pain at that moment was roughly equal to the pain that resulted from the relapse.

3. The pain that resulted from the relapse was far worse than the pain at the moment I said "Dammit" and relapsed.

Write down how you feel as you answer these questions, comparing your pain at the moment you said "Dammit" to the pain you experienced as a result of saying it and picking up that first drink/drug? Write down your sensations, as best you can.

_____

_____

_____

_____

You are, in fact, the person who has suffered and is suffering painful sensations that would not have occurred if you had not said "Dammit" and taken the first drink/drug. These sensations include both your own pain and the pain of knowing how much suffering you may have caused others.

Imagine the person you are today, who has suffered these painful sensations and is probably still suffering them, going back in time and talking to the person you were, with all the pain you were in, just before you said "Dammit" and picked up the first drink/drug. Write down anything and everything that you would like him or her to hear before taking that first drink/drug.

_____

_____

_____

_____

Now write down what you think she or he would have said in response.

_____

_____

_____

_____

Write down any sensations or understanding you experienced while answering questions that compare the pain before saying "Dammit" with the pain of the consequences that followed. Share with a partner and/or group.

_____

_____

_____

_____

Rate how much you agree with the following quotation from the *AA Big Book* as it applies to your experience of the "Dammit" relapse:

"…when we began to drink…there was little serious or effective thought during the period of premeditation of what the terrific consequences might be."

1. Not at all   2. Slightly   3. Moderately   4. Totally

Again, think about all the things you have read, heard, or experienced with 12 Step Recovery so far. If you are new to the program and/or to this realization, do not fret for a second if you can't think of much. Just ask yourself if you are open the group's answers, and how they might apply to you. Write down ways that 12 Step Recovery helps us to keep track of the painful consequences of saying "Dammit," even when some particular person, place, or thing has us painfully frustrated. Specifically:

- How does the program help us remember the painful consequences we have already suffered and those we are likely to suffer, even when the frustration of one or more important things fills mind and body with sensations that seem so painful the only way to relieve them seems to be saying "Dammit" and taking that first drink/drug? (Write your thoughts below.)

_____

_____

_____

_____

- What tools and/or principles do you already know about? Share any that have helped you remember the consequences and resist saying "Dammit" in the past, even if you did eventually drink/drug again. Share any tools you know about which would have helped on the day you said "Dammit." Share any change in willingness to use these tools to prevent yourself from saying "Dammit" and relapsing ever again.

_____

_____

_____

_____

- When you experience sensations which make it seem like it is just too painful to care about anything except relief, what does 12 Step Recovery suggest you do about those sensations? What sensations does the program promise if you do what it suggests? Does anyone in the group have experience of that truth? Share and discuss.

_____

_____

_____

_____

Rate how much you agree with the following:

Part B of Realization Number Three—not caring about what WILL happen—has increased my understanding of the need to remember, especially when I'm upset, how much I suffer from the real consequences of saying "dammit" and taking that first drink/drug.

1. Not at all   2. Slightly   3. Moderately   4. Totally

EXPLETIVE ("DAMMIT") RELAPSE REALIZATION NUMBER FOUR

Picture yourself any of the times you said "Dammit" and picked up the first drink/drug of relapse. Regardless of your actual age, how many years old did you feel emotionally at that moment? (Circle one.)

0-3

4-6

7-9

10-12

13-15

16-18

19-21

22-25

older than 25 but less than my actual age

my actual age

older than my actual age

Regardless of your feeling at that moment, how would you now rate your actions and/or attitude when you said "Dammit" and drank/drugged? (Circle the most accurate description.)

✓ appropriate to my years and wisdom

✓ foolish, perhaps, but adult

✓ less mature than I would expect of someone my age

✓ downright childish

Rate how much you agree with the following:

"When I say 'Dammit' and pick up the first drink/drug, I am, in effect, having a temper tantrum."

1. Not at all   2. Slightly   3. Moderately   4. Totally

Shame check: If you chose anything other than number 1, how reluctant would you be to share this truth about your immaturity with the important people in your life, assuming they do not have an alcohol or drug problem and they know that you do?

1. Not at all   2. Slightly   3. Moderately   4. Extremely   5. N.A.

As you look at this, share your answers, thoughts, and feelings with a partner/group. Notice similarities as well as changes in group energy. Share your perceptions of these things.

Rate your agreement with the following:

"Apparently, I will have to find a way to 'grow up' and/or maintain an adult reaction to life, no matter what happens, if I am to avoid yet another 'Dammit' relapse."

1. Not at all   2. Slightly   3. Moderately   4. Totally

Complete: "My idea of how to do this is…

_____

_____

_____

_____

_____."

My confidence I can "grow up" all by myself is (circle one. 10 is supreme confidence and 1 is little or none):

1   2   3   4   5   6   7   8   9   10

My confidence I can maintain my adult reactions all by myself is:

1   2   3   4   5   6   7   8   9   10

My willingness to submit to a "transformational process," to actually work at changing myself in the direction of more maturity is (circle one. 10 is willingness to go to any length and 1 is little or none):

1   2   3   4   5   6   7   8   9   10

Share your answers to this last set of questions, along with your reactions while answering them.

Again, think about all the things you have read, heard, or experienced with 12 Step Recovery so far. If you are new to the program and/or to this realization, do not fret for a second if you can't think of much. Just ask yourself if you are open to the group's answers and to how they might apply to you. Write down ways that 12 Step Recovery helps us to "grow up," even when some particular person, place, or thing may make us want to say "Dammit!" or the like, throw a tantrum like a three-year-old, and take that first drink/drug. Specifically:

- How does the program help us reduce our immature reactions at the same time we are growing and maintaining more mature ones?

  _____

  _____

  _____

  _____

- What tools and/or principles do you already know about? Share any that have helped you react more maturely and not say "Dammit" in the past, even if you did eventually drink/drug again. Share any tools you know about which would have helped on the day you said "Dammit!" Share any change in willingness to use these tools to prevent yourself from saying "Dammit" and relapsing ever again.

  _____

  _____

  _____

  _____

- When you experience sensations which feel like the abandonment or rage of a child, what does 12 Step Recovery suggest you do about those sensations? What sensations does the program promise if you do what it suggests? Does anyone in the group have experience of that truth? Share and discuss.

  _____

  _____

  _____

  _____

Rate how much you agree with the following:

Realization Number Four about the "Dammit" relapse—the emotional age at which I sometimes react—has increased my understanding of the need to grow up emotionally if I am not to (again) say "Dammit" and take that first drink/drug.

1. Not at all   2. Slightly   3. Moderately   4. Totally

That part of me which reacts like a child may need regular emotional support to never (again) say "Dammit" and take that first drink/drug.

1. Not at all   2. Slightly   3. Moderately   4. Totally

Self-Assessment

Review your work on the four realizations about the expletive/"Dammit" relapse. Then complete the following ratings and/or sentences.

Rate how much you agree with the following statement:

"In doing these four sections on the expletive relapse, I feel that my eyes have been opened about what is really going on when I say 'Dammit' and pick up the first drink/drug."

1. Not at all   2. Slightly   3. Moderately   4. Totally

The realization that felt the most emotional was (circle one):

1. That I actually seem unable to cope with reality/adult life without chemicals.

2. That I am a "quitter" when I say "Dammit" and pick up the first drink/drug.

3. That I forget/deny what I really care about when saying "Dammit" and picking up the first drink/drug.

4. That I am unable to see or remember the real consequences of saying "Dammit" and picking up the first drink/drug.

5. That my "Dammit" is the reaction of a child not getting his or her own way.

The realization that most changed how I think about addiction and recovery was (circle one):

1. That I actually seem unable to cope with reality/adult life without chemicals.

2. That I am a "quitter" when I say "Dammit" and pick up the first drink/drug.

3. That I forget/deny what I really care about when saying "Dammit" and picking up the first drink/drug.

4. That I am unable to see or remember the real consequences of saying "Dammit" and picking up the first drink/drug.

5. That my "Dammit" is the reaction of a child not getting his or her own way.

As a result of what I now "get" about the "Dammit" relapse and the thinking behind it, I am more likely to (circle all that apply):

1. Attend peer support meetings and aftercare if it is available.

2. Attend 12 Step meetings.

3. Get a sponsor.

4. Attend 90 meetings in 90 days.

5. Remain clean and sober.

6. Continue individual counseling or psychotherapy

7. Be working at my recovery one year from now, including peer support groups.

8. Be working at my recovery three years from now, including peer support groups

9. Be working at my recovery ten years from now, including peer support groups.

10. Really work to find some form of spiritual experience or transformation.

11. Other:

Share and discuss.

ANONYMOUS MAINTENANCE PLAN SCALE: AFTER YOU FINISH THE WORKBOOK

This page is an anonymous survey, designed to collect results for the whole group. It tries to measure how much difference the workbook/group is making overall. You were asked to choose one "plan" before you started the workbook and after Part I. An honest answer on this scale will make the workbook better for others over the long haul. Other questions inside the workbook gave you a chance to assess and discuss how it has been working for you and your group.

Do not put your name on this page---it is meant to be cut out and handed in.

Your counselor may ask you all to put a date or some other mark on the page so s/he knows which group s/he is recording. S/he will calculate only the average numbers for your group.

Below are five possible ways to maintain your own recovery after completing this workbook and any program of which it is a part. Please, circle the one that most closely describes what you are likely to do after you finish the workbook and the program, even if the description is not perfect.

The closest description of my plan to stay clean and sober after completing this program:

1. None. I plan to return to the use of alcohol and/or drugs.

2. Just stay away from drugs and alcohol, using my willpower.

3. Start or resume at least one activity, such as exercise, a nutritional program, a new hobby, or even more time working, to "stay busy" or "keep me going" (without returning to alcohol/drugs). I will not involve myself with any sort of "mutual help" group.

4. Whether I also do parts of number 3 or not, I will attend some sort of "mutual help" meetings until I feel "out of the woods" and able to stay off drugs/alcohol on my own. Or I might participate in some form of psychotherapy until I think I am ready to stay clean and sober on my own. Or I will stay clean and sober solely through my religion, without participation in groups or activities specifically for recovering alcoholic/addicts.

5. Even if I also do some of the above, I will join a 12 Step Program, get a sponsor, work the steps, and attend meetings. If I have already started this, I will continue under the guidance of my sponsor.

19408797R00035

Made in the USA
Charleston, SC
22 May 2013